Choral Conducting

BY

ARCHIBALD T. DAVISON

Professor of Choral Music, Harvard University

CAMBRIDGE, MASSACHUSETTS
HARVARD UNIVERSITY PRESS
1954

Seventh Printing

LONDON : GEOFFREY CUMBERLEGE
OXFORD UNIVERSITY PRESS

PRINTED AT THE HARVARD UNIVERSITY PRINTING OFFICE
CAMBRIDGE, MASS., U. S. A.

To

THE MULTITUDE OF SINGERS

WHOSE FORBEARANCE AND COÖPERATION THROUGH MANY YEARS

HAVE AIDED ME IN FORMULATING

THE PRINCIPLES LAID DOWN IN THIS BOOK

PREFACE

Having completed some thirty-five years of choral conducting, and being now on the point of giving myself over to the enjoyment of music which it has not been my duty to prepare for public performance, I am venturing to set down my own convictions regarding good choral singing and to record the methods by which I have tried to make those ideals articulate. To many, my way with a chorus will seem extreme, even fantastic, perhaps, and I can well believe that few will care to try it. But, for me, one of the real satisfactions of choral work has issued from the gradual building up of a technique which is my own, the product of experiment and the consummation of my artistic beliefs.

If this book has any value, then, it will not be for the veteran conductor whose opinions, already fixed, I have no slightest wish to alter; it will be for the beginner to whom my experience may offer some aid, particularly in those matters which concern the relations between conductor and chorus, relations upon which success so greatly depends. Where technical matters are concerned, I would urge no one to accept my viewpoint unless, after adequate trial, he finds reason to agree with me.

To Sir Adrian Boult, conductor of the orchestra and chorus of the British Broadcasting Corporation, I express my heartiest thanks for his painstaking reading of the text, as well as for many valuable suggestions.

In the illustrations, as in the book, I have necessarily omitted much, being content to stress details which seem to me to be of prime importance. If I have contributed anything that is helpful to the untried choral conductor, I shall be happy indeed.

A. T. D.

Cambridge
February 10, 1940

CONTENTS

CONTENTS

CHAPTER I

THE CONDUCTOR

THE CONDUCTOR whose activities are confined to the field of choral music is frequently looked down upon as a musician with a professional equipment so limited that it denies him a major role in any large musical enterprise, and automatically relegates him to the unenviable status of a musical specialist. The very term "choral conductor" is sometimes used to suggest a lack of those varied capacities which it is taken for granted a thoroughgoing musician should possess, and this derogation is, alas, too often a just one. The choral conductor "type" is a familiar feature of amateur musical effort. He conquers by personality rather than by musicianship. His acquaintance with the literature of music is far too small, and his resourcefulness in making available a wide variety of works lacks the support of scholarship. His sense of discrimination between good and bad music is generally intuitive because it has not been trained, and he crowns all by disregarding the canons of conducting as musicians know them, substituting therefor a system of his own made up of interpretative gestures which are meaningful only to his own group.

It is, perhaps, because we as choral conductors deal mainly with amateurs and with amateur musical psychology that more has not been demanded of us. This is unfortunate, for it is the amateur who, above all, needs the stimulus which can only be offered by thoroughly competent training; and proof that such direction alone will produce the best results from an organization of untrained singers may be found by comparing the achievement of the average choral conductor with the accomplishment of one who represents everything that we mean by the word "musicianship."

First of all, the choral conductor should have a well-trained ear, quick to detect the many and varied departures from musical accuracy of which even the best choruses are sometimes guilty. Solfège supplies the highest schooling in this particular, but even a simple, systematic course in ear-training will reinforce a department in which many of us are seriously deficient. Without a scientifically trained ear, the choral conductor is at a permanent and serious disadvantage; even with the possession of an acute and discriminating aural sense, the beginner will fail to hear much that is important. Self-consciousness and concern with manifold detail — much of it almost mechanical — will so turn him in upon himself that bad tone, flatting, insecure singing, and even wrong notes will not pierce the armor of his preoccupation. At first, he may be — and often is — quite satisfied if the music simply goes on. Page after page will pass by, filled with a multitude of choral shortcomings of which he may be vaguely aware; some instinct tells him, perhaps, that all is not well, but he is helpless, hypnotized by the mere continuity of the music, and he fears to interrupt it, both because he has only a foggy idea of what is wrong and because, if he stops, he must face two of the beginner's most dreaded problems, finding a convenient place to recommence, and after that, putting the music in motion. Little by little the more intrusive errors will force themselves upon him until gradually he will come to hear not the parts, but the whole, correcting not only technical faults, but instructing in matters of style as well. And when, after long experience of choral music and of singers and their ways, he gains that sixth sense which enables him to detect mistakes *before* they are made, listening not only with the ear, but also with the imagination, he will have attained the full stature of a conductor at least insofar as that indispensable member, a highly trained ear, is concerned.

It would seem that the foregoing might have been taken for granted, so necessary is a sensitive and discriminating ear; there are, however, less obvious essentials, one of which is a knowledge of matters orchestral. It is not pleasant to think how many of us are limited by woeful incompetence in this department. Many works are scored for both orchestra and chorus; in some the instrumental factor is almost if not quite as important as the choral, and a musicianly rehearsing and performance of such works presupposes attainments outside the strictly choral field.[1] Of these, score-reading is certainly one. Few of us, it is to be feared, experience the same degree of confidence when conducting from a "full" score that we feel when dealing with the lucidities of a "vocal" edition. Yet intelligent mastery of a composition, a full comprehension of all that it contains, and the final production of a complete and musicianly rendition depend in the beginning on an understanding of everything that the composer has written down, and on the power to transmit that knowledge clearly and readily from the full score at rehearsals and performances.

Indeed, there is no musical fallacy so common to the uninitiated — unless it be that organ and piano technique are identical — as the delusion that anyone who can train an orchestra can train a chorus, and *vice versa*. The physical motions by which both bodies are led are, to be sure, identical, but the

---

[1] Expert *a cappella* singing is doubtless the final test of a choral conductor's skill; but in many instances where the orchestra is joined with the chorus, especially in eighteenth-century works, extensive modifications in unaccompanied choral style must be made. These concern pronunciation, tone, and many other details, and it is the task of the choral conductor to apply these modifications wisely. Each composition requires separate consideration in this regard, and each composition must be studied with reference to its total effectiveness. The style of the music, the orchestration, and the balance of importance between orchestra and chorus are germane to the question. One does not, for example, follow the same methods of chorus training for the B minor Mass, the *German Requiem*, the *Israel in Egypt*, and *The Blessed Damosel*.

methods by which each is brought to a state of proficiency are quite unlike. The orchestral conductor is frequently at a loss as to how to produce a certain choral effect, and similarly, the choral conductor is too often unable to achieve anything like finesse in the instrumental part of a choral work. Most orchestral conductors depend on the leader of the chorus to prepare the choral parts of a work for them, but the choral conductor, contemplating a performance involving both voices and instruments to be directed by himself, must assume entire responsibility. We should not rely, as we so often do, on the tolerance and good will of professional orchestral players to compensate for our own deficiencies. This is not to say that choral conductors need aspire to a competence that is born of almost daily contact with orchestral forces, but they should understand the technique and capacity of each instrument, should be able to adjust the balance of sonorities both within the orchestra itself and in conjunction with the chorus, and should have at least an adequate idea of how good orchestral results are obtained. In return for such knowledge, and the tactful exercise of it, the choral conductor may justly expect the sympathetic professional coöperation of the orchestra.

In addition to the study of score-reading, then, the choral conductor should take a practical course in orchestral training; and this work he should pursue up to a point where he can effectively direct all the forces involved and command the respect of all the participants.

But even more than the regard of his co-workers, the choral conductor should esteem his own self-respect as a musician. Many, of course, do achieve measurable results without benefit of those branches of knowledge which do not appear to bear directly on choral training; yet their possession adds to efficiency in untold ways. "What," it may be asked, "is to be gained by a study of musical theory, of form, of harmony and counterpoint? Are these not the composer's business, and, if so, why should it be necessary for the conductor to concern himself with such details?" The answer is, of course, that an understanding of these branches of music is an essential part of the equipment of every interpreter. The composer is justified in expecting of the conductor an intelligent approach to the technical elements of which his music consists. He furnishes those elements "ready-to-wear" as it were. It remains for the conductor to make those elements articulate; and without a reasonably thorough knowledge of them he cannot properly discharge his responsibility.

Even more important, however, is familiarity with the history of music, especially that part of it which deals with musical literature and styles. More than instinct is needed as a guide to the interpretation of Haydn as a composer different from Palestrina. To present the works of various eras, or even the works of two musicians of the same era, a conductor should familiarize himself with the idiom of each composer as it appears not in one but in many works, setting that idiom, thereafter, against the background of the technical and aesthetic canons of its age.

On the practical side, some ability as a pianist is desirable as well as an intelligent command of the singing voice. In neither field is virtuosity implied, particularly in the case of singing, for there a trained voice is, on the whole, a drawback. There are instances when the leader can instruct much more quickly from the keyboard than from the podium, as, for example, in the early stages of teaching a new and difficult piece, when with even the best accompanists there is bound to be a time-lag where there are frequent corrections. A conductor with a professionally trained voice will more often than not defeat his own intentions because the chorus, not being vocally expert as he is, will nevertheless attempt to match the luster of his illustrations, an especially disastrous type of emulation which can only end by producing the distorted vocal quality inevitable in such circumstances. The effort to superimpose mass voice instruction on a large group is most unwise, partly because all such teaching involving placement, breath-control, etc., must be applied individually to be effective, and partly because there is no time for any extended drill outside the rehearsing of the music. The conductor does not need to assume the singing teacher's function; all that is necessary is an expressive, well-controlled voice, a kind of common denominator of amateur singing raised to the nth power, with which he is enabled to demonstrate to the chorus what he expects from them in return.

While adequate vocal illustration by the conductor may be considered as an essential in chorus training, that is by no means its only virtue. It appreciably diminishes the psychological distance between director and chorus; it makes — or appears to make — instruction much less categorical and, by establishing a reciprocal basis for the work, goes far towards creating that identity of spirit which is requisite to the whole project. To say that conductor and chorus must be in sympathy is not enough. They must be *one*. The conductor should enter into every problem not only as conductor, but as chorister also; sometimes, quite instinctively, he even breathes with his singers, a symbol of his unity with them and of his vigilance in their behalf. Once that unity is established, the chorus, on its part, may be counted on to return a prompt and coöperative response to the conductor's efforts. There are some musicians, alas, who clearly never should have followed the career of choral conducting; they lack the ability to teach, or they suffer from a short-circuited personality to such an extent that they are incapable of a sympathetic approach to their charges. Yet one assumes a grave responsibility in discouraging an unpromising beginner; hopes that he will surmount his personal shortcomings and will blossom forth into an evocative and inspired leader are now and again realized. But without hesitation I should advise anyone who, because of physical limitations, will never be able to express himself provocatively through his singing voice to abandon the study of choral conducting.

Of all the factors, musical and personal, which serve to bring about a community of spirit between conductor and chorus, none is more powerful than the exercise of spontaneous humor. It would be possible to build up an equation having on one side a number of separate qualities which a choral conductor will find indispensable — tact, insight, naturalness of manner, and enthusiasm, for example — and on the other simply humor. But that humor must be subjective as well as objective. The conductor himself, if he is absorbed in his work, will often quite innocently say or do things which amuse the chorus. He suffers no loss of prestige by laughing at himself or even by mimicking himself. A rehearsal should be enjoyable in the widest sense. The conductor or singer who does not anticipate the fun as well as the artistic profit should stay at home. During the course of an hour and a half's rehearsal a score of occasions will arise which suggest some display of humor on the conductor's part, and if those occasions are lost the rehearsal is just so much less a stimulating human enterprise. To take advantage of such occasions is not to waste time; the telling of a story, the interchange of good-humored comment between chorus and conductor, these are the natural accompaniments of a live rehearsal, and they are rewarded by a quickened interest and by better singing.

It should be remembered, too, that the conducting of an amateur chorus is no occupation for the lazy man. The "armchair" leader who monotonously intones page, line, and measure numbers, who issues only the necessary corrections and suggestions, and who remains unexcited and impersonal, is inevitably rewarded by "arm-chair" singing. Conducting an amateur chorus is like throwing a rubber ball at a stone wall. There is as much rebound as there is force in the throw. A certain amount of physical exertion must be taken for granted; the easygoing conductor who prefers to sit rather than stand through a rehearsal, and who spares himself every physical exertion, not only encourages uninterested singing, but he tempts himself, as well, to an attitude of mental laziness which causes him to overlook many faults and to disregard many opportunities for the exercise of his ingenuity.

How much a conductor needs ingenuity will be many times suggested in the pages which follow — not alone the type of ingenuity which finds the best way out of a difficult "local" situation having to do with the temperamental frailties of human nature, the vocal limitations of the earnest but untutored singer, or with the physical conditions that accompany the choral setting, rehearsal room, seating, etc., but more especially the kind of ingenuity that may be termed "an ear for effect" — how, in short, to see behind the notes and words all the possibilities of creating vivid artistic moments. These, neither the composer nor the publisher can indicate. They are hidden in the material of almost every choral page, and they are evident only to him who is ingenious and imaginative. In their higher phases they amount sometimes to sheer invention. Of invention, necessity is invariably cited as the unique parent; but the frankly biological derivation of that old saying demands completion, and as having a just claim to paternity I heartily recommend the truly resourceful conductor.

Finally, there are few imaginable enterprises so enthralling as the directing of an amateur chorus. To have companionship with eager men and women whose joy it is to create beauty by breathing life and significance into music which without the exercise of their skill and intelligence would remain cold symbols on a printed page; to have a part with them in the mutual accomplishment of high artistic ends arrived at only after enthusiastic coöperation and painstaking labor; to see them grow in sensitiveness to the refinements of performance and in the appreciation of what is true and enduring in art — I cannot believe that many occupations offer greater rewards.

CHAPTER II

THE BEAT

THE GESTURES of time-beating are traditional. Conductors should scrupulously adhere to that tradition by employing the customary motions, and choruses should be instructed to obey those motions without question. No one would expect an intelligent response to obscure verbal commands. Why therefore should a chorus be required unfailingly to interpret haphazard gesticulations which may never be twice alike and which succeed only because the singers have rehearsed sufficiently to enable them to keep together? Even casual association with an orchestra will speedily inform those whom Gustav Holst used to call "stick-waggers" that to deal in anything but the common currency of time-beating will speedily end in chaos.

It is primarily for the purpose of setting the rhythm and as an aid to interpretation that gestures are employed; but they ought not to serve either purpose exclusively for any length of time, and they are most valuable when they represent a combination of both. Their mastery ought first to be gained by means of private practice, for the beginner's motions should, as soon as possible, become automatic. No leader can bestow his full attention on the singing if he must give thought to the direction in which his hand ought next to move.[1]

[1] Practice before a mirror is exceedingly valuable, as it shows the conductor whether or not his beat is clear and definite, and at the same time enables him to avoid the awkward, angular motions of which he would otherwise be unaware. Practice should not, however, be too long divorced from music. After the mechanics have been mastered, the student should sing while he conducts.

All this would seem to imply that the canons of conducting are relatively inflexible, and that is true. This does not mean, however, that the conductor is to behave like a human metronome. When the music suggests it, he may depart from routine method for purposes of emphasis or suggestion, but such gestures will be occasional and will be the more effective because they are rare.[2] Where there is no rhythmic complication present in the music the conductor may even cease beating for the space of a few measures. Indeed, some degree of elasticity is inherent in such details as time-beating. Its indications are but means to an end, and a too arbitrary application of them is bound to result in something mechanical rather than artistic.

In the beginning one would do well to try conducting both with and without baton, continuing both methods until experience decides which is the more satisfactory. To some conductors greater freedom and expressiveness seem possible if both hands are disengaged; to others the stick is a guarantee of precision. One practical advantage that rests with the baton-less conductor is that he can stop the chorus more promptly by clapping the hands sharply than by tapping his stick on the music rack. With a large chorus singing forte the latter method is often quite ineffective, whereas the former never fails to produce silence immediately. But whether or not a baton is used, the beginner should be warned against the consistent use of *both* hands. If the time is beaten with the right hand, the left may sometimes accompany it, but, in general, the left hand should be kept in reserve to indicate dynamics, crescendi, diminuendi, and sforzandi, and to fill a host of useful offices interpretative and otherwise.

Particularly important to the chorus is the preliminary or "warning" beat which directly precedes the first "singing" beat

---

[2] For many reasons very few liberties should be taken with the first beat of the measure. Singers and particularly orchestral players rely on the inevitable recurrence of a down beat to introduce each new bar.

and which is a sign for the chorus to breathe in and in other ways to prepare to attack. That beat is, in duration, the exact equivalent of the following, or first actual beat of the piece. If, for example, the meter is 4/4 and the piece begins on the third beat of the measure, the conductor will indicate an imaginary second beat as a warning:

EXAMPLE I

Although one can offer no good reason why a chorus should not attack when the time to sing arrives, the experienced choral conductor generally prefers to make assurance trebly sure by reinforcing the "singing" beat by a slight elevation of the shoulders and a little forward inclination of the head.

Of scarcely less significance is the closing or release gesture. When the final note is held, the "cut-off" sign is usually made in one of two ways: the conductor either moves his hand to the left at a moderate pace, to notify the chorus that the release will follow at once, making immediately thereafter a quick sweeping gesture to the right to indicate the actual "cut-off"; or he reverses the direction of the motions, moving first to the right and then to the left. In either case, it is the first of the two signs which is, on the whole, the more important; that sign must be of sufficient duration to prepare the chorus for the final indication.[8]

There is a principle of choral conducting which applies not only to warning beats but also to rests and other pauses in the music, namely, that all such signs be indicated by the conductor

[8] Choristers sometimes object that a conductor, by the suddenness of his release gesture, causes them to "bite their tongues."

as unobtrusively as possible. Actually there is no reason why a rest should not be beaten as violently as the musical context would suggest, and if one were dealing with professional orchestral players, for example, the amount of energy expended would be productive of no mishap. But under like circumstances amateur choristers will sometimes be misled into singing when the music calls for silence.

No single treatise could contain the thousand and one small practical devices by which the conductor puts the chorus at its ease, inspires confidence, and makes himself articulate. These only discover themselves in the course of many rehearsals and concerts. The young conductor will learn that to wait an appreciable moment before the attack, to look over the singers, perhaps to smile at them, to establish somehow a feeling of anticipation that something memorable is about to happen, go far towards insuring a good beginning. He will learn, too, that accompanying every sixteenth note with a separate gesture merely confuses the chorus; that if he teaches his singers to follow a clean and decisive beat the sixteenth notes will take care of themselves. But he will learn these and many more details only after much disheartening experience.

TABLE OF BEATS

On page 15 is a table for beating the commonly employed meters. In a few cases alternate diagrams might be offered, but those here presented conform, I believe, to customary practice.[4]

It will be observed that the first beat (primary accent) is downward, and that the secondary accent is toward the right. These accents are the crucial rhythmical incidents of the measure and when they occur the conductor's hand or stick must

---

[4] Should the student wish to consult additional diagrams he will find them in *A Handbook on the Technique of Conducting*, by Adrian C. Boult (Hall, Ltd., Oxford), *The Technic of the Baton*, by Albert Stoessel (Fischer, 1920), and *Conducting and Orchestral Routine*, by Frank E. Kendrie (H. W. Gray Co., 1930).

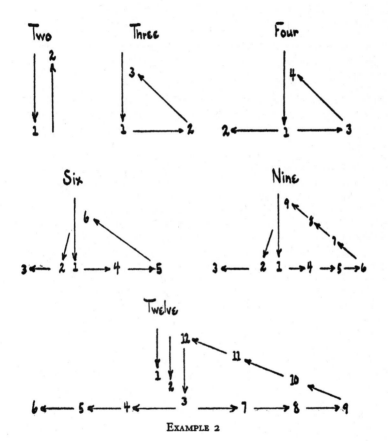

EXAMPLE 2

be clearly within the vision of the chorus. If the time is beaten in the accepted way no misunderstanding can arise.[5]

Treatment of the more unusual meters such as 5/4 and 7/4 is a more subtle matter. It is evident from the barring of their music that many composers look upon 5 as a combination of 3 and 2, and on 7 as a combination of 3 and 4. Many conductors, too, accept this point of view. Thus 5 and 7 are frequently beaten as indicated in Example 4 (pages 17 and 18).

Two details will be noted, first that the secondary accent is marked by a down beat much shorter than that used to indicate the first or primary beat of the measure, and second that the position of the secondary accents is not uniform, practice depending on the accentuation of the text.

For the sensitive conductor, however, the foregoing represents a far too inflexible method. For him there are rhythmical refinements within the bar which call for a less categorical manipulation of the beat. Two down beats within a bar, however much they may be contrasted in length, mean two *accents*; and the tendency, in singing, is to respond to any down beat by a marked stress. This may result in an unnatural scansion of a line that in reality possesses but one marked accent. Furthermore, the secondary stresses may fall on any beat within the bar except the first one, a fact that makes any preconceived

[5] A rare exception to tradition is occasionally to be observed in the opera house, where 4/4 is beaten in this way:

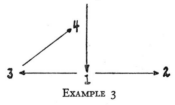

EXAMPLE 3

The reason is obvious; if customary procedure were followed the third beat or secondary accent would be less easy to identify because of the dim lighting; whereas if the third beat is carried to the left the baton stands out sharply against the conductor's white shirt-front.

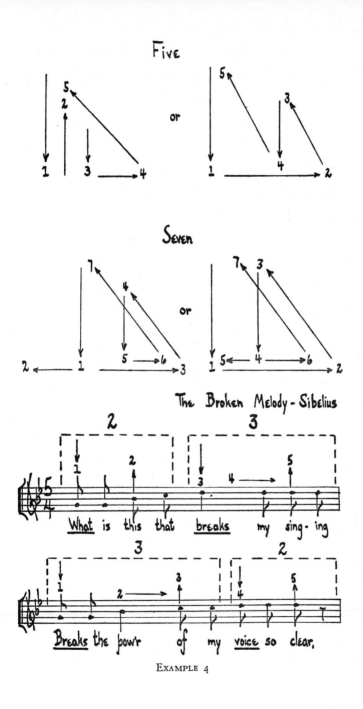

EXAMPLE 4

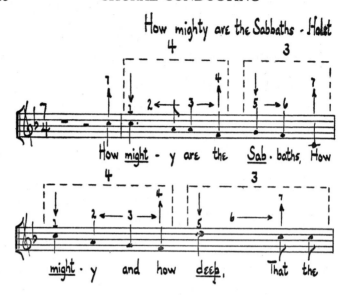

EXAMPLE 4 CONT.

scheme of beating impracticable. In speaking the lines accompanying the music given above, one would be guilty of distorting the poetical flow if he delivered the words thus:

> *What* is this that *breaks* my singing,
> *Breaks* the power of my *voice* so clear. . . .

Rather he would declaim this passage:

> *What* is this that breaks my singing,
> *Breaks* the power of my voice so clear. . . .

So, in order to preserve the normal text accentuation when it is conditioned by the accompaniment of music, many conductors treat 7's and 5's with appropriate elasticity. Thus the foregoing passages would be treated by many conductors as shown in Example 5 (pages 19 and 20).

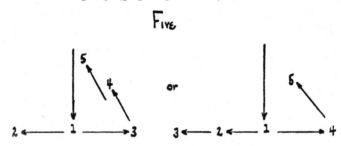

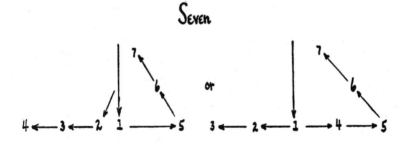

EXAMPLE 5

EXAMPLE 5 CONT.

In the conducting of unbarred music such as plainsong and of barred music whose measures are so long that a time-signature is not feasible, the best method is to indicate the beginning of each new bar by a decided down beat, stressing the other accented words or syllables by a shorter motion in the same direction (Example 6).[6]

[6] The following, some of which are represented in the musical illustrations in these pages, will be found profitable for the study of conducting the less common meters:

How Mighty are the Sabbaths (unison version), Holst (Boosey and Hawkes)

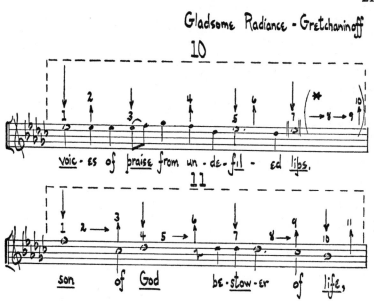

EXAMPLE 6

All the foregoing tables are predicated on the assumption that the tempo is sufficiently moderate to allow one beat to each unit within the bar. But in the case of a rapid tempo one beat to the unit is often not practicable and sometimes impossible. Under such conditions the method must be fore-

Rise up, my Love, my Fair One, Willan (Oxford University Press)
Magnificat and *Nunc Dimittis*, Vaughan Williams (J. Curwen and Sons)
The Broken Melody, Sibelius (G. Schirmer)
Gladsome Radiance, Gretchaninoff (The H. W. Gray Co.)
Hymn to Agni, Holst (Stainer and Bell)
A Spotless Rose, Howells (Stainer and Bell)
Of one that is so fair and bright, Holst (J. Curwen and Sons)
Lullay my Liking, Holst (J. Curwen and Sons).

shortened, and often only the main and secondary accents in the bar are indicated. For example, in rapid 4/4 or 6/8 or in 2/2 (*alla breve*) two beats in a bar are generally used as in simple 2/4. In rapid 3/4 one down beat suffices. Rapid 9/4 is beaten like 3/4 and 12/4 like 4/4.[7] The same principle holds true for the unusual meters. Rapid 5/4, depending on the location of the secondary accent, is frequently presented as follows:

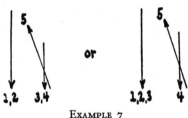

EXAMPLE 7

Where the tempo is too slow to admit of the convenient use of one beat to each unit of the bar, the beats are simply subdivided as follows:

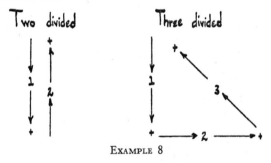

EXAMPLE 8

This system is also useful when dealing with retards, where preserving the unit in a passage of which the tempo becomes

[7] Before the sixteenth century the "tactus" had been adopted as a definite indication of tempo; and for some time thereafter the performer was left in no doubt as to the composer's intentions regarding pace. Now it is the equivocal "tempo mark" which is used. So, although in each case I have used the

progressively slower would result in complete indefiniteness of
gesture. The following method of beating is recommended:

EXAMPLE 9

No diagram can adequately represent all the conductor's
motions, especially the inevitable loops and dips that join them
together; indeed, except for preserving the traditional direction of each beat and giving the chorus due notice that he is
about to move from one beat to the next, the conductor is
entirely governed by the musical situation of the moment. It
would, of course, be more life-like to depict the normal four-
beat bar not in consistently straight lines, but as follows:

quarter note as the unit, it goes without saying that in our modern system of
notation it is the *tempo mark* and not the unit of beat which conditions the
conductor's gestures. Thus measures of 4/2, 4/4, 4/8, and 4/16 may, depending on the tempo mark, be of equal length in performance.

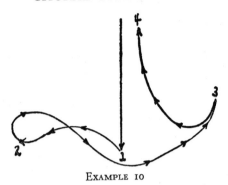

EXAMPLE 10

But on the whole, the most necessary part of the young conductor's knowledge of time-beating is that which concerns
the *direction* of each beat. If his coördination is normal and if
he is not unregenerately awkward, he may count on it that the
chorus will find his gestures intelligible.

CHAPTER III

THE CHORUS

CHORUSES are of three kinds: women's voices, men's voices, and mixed voices. The first two suffer in common from a number of limitations, including the comparatively small range which separates even the extreme notes of the outer voices, and the absence of varied tonal color that results from uniformity of timbre. Counterpoint is the life of choral music, but because of the conditions stated above the only element in counterpoint that is conspicuous in music for men's or women's voices is the rhythmic one. Almost any melody will eventually spread itself over a fair compass, and if it is a really independent melody it will be frequently invading the range of its neighbor parts; in fact, the kaleidoscopic changes of color which result from voice-crossing and from the exploitation of the various sections of its range by a single choral part go far to compensate for those limitations which beset even choral music for mixed voices. But first and second tenors (or first and second sopranos) and the lower parts as well are so similar in tone that counterpoint is virtually wasted on them. This has resulted, in the case of men's voices, in a mass of harmonic writing, much of it of the lush variety invited by a rich and often cloying texture, and in the case of women's voices in an emphasis not only on harmony but on the use of accompaniment as well. Men's voices are at least substantial and self-supporting; women's voices are not, because in the absence of masculine coöperation they lack what an accompaniment can supply, namely the indispensable bass or musical foundation.

In the orchestral field there are to be found compositions

for a single family of instruments, say for horns and trombones, or flutes and clarinets. But these pieces are occasional and one would hesitate to spend an evening devoted only, let us say, to music for four 'cellos. By the same token anyone who has attended concerts of music written exclusively for men's or women's chorus must realize that such music is most effective when it serves as a contrast to something else.

Another serious defect of these special groups is that the greatest choral composers have, to an extent that is significant, passed them by. Indeed, the amount of really good music written originally for these two media is amazingly small; hence their programs are likely to be of inferior quality, or made up of arrangements which are too often aesthetic monstrosities to be avoided if it is possible.

To tilt against the abnormal phenomenon of this musical segregation of the sexes would be no more than a rhetorical gesture. The fact has become too deeply rooted in American life. Clubs, societies, guilds, professions, and athletic pursuits may operate more beneficially by limiting their membership to men or women. But art is indifferent to these considerations; it ignores persons and social theories, and, whether by chance or design, it has decreed that its highest fulfillment in terms of choral music shall take the form of music for mixed voices. When a conductor undertakes to organize a chorus within the community, and, finding himself free to choose, elects to establish a chorus of men or women, he is setting his face squarely against the accepted canons of musical art.

The mixed chorus is free of the technical disadvantages of which I have been speaking; it affords every resource available to voices in combination. Its *a cappella* literature is extensive and varied; and in music for mixed voices and instruments composers have found a medium for the expression of unsurpassed eloquence.[1] It is not to be denied, I believe, that music

[1] If your chorus is a small one, or even if it is reasonably large, make an

for mixed chorus is, both for participants and audience, im-
measurably more profitable and rewarding than that for any
other group of voices.

Thirty years ago, if one were contemplating a performance
of Bach's *Magnificat* or Hindemith's *Das Unaufhörliche* (had
it then been in existence), he would have recruited his chorus
from the ranks of experienced singers, with emphasis on trained
voices and able sight-readers: in other words on veteran choristers most of whom would have been between thirty and sixty
years of age. The reverse is now quite generally the case, for
we have learned that a group of young, enthusiastic singers in
their late teens and early twenties can perform the most difficult music more impressively than their elders.[2] I have never
paid much attention to the "quality" of a choral candidate's
voice. I am much more influenced by the extent of his desire
to sing, and by his interest in music.[3]

In the first place, trained singers find it both difficult and

---

effort to interest it in the considerable and too generally neglected field of
unison (or octave) and three-part music. A curious and damaging prejudice
exists against singing in anything less than four parts; but for the chorus
which is deficient in some one part (usually tenors and occasionally altos)
music in more modest groupings is often a solution. Take, for example, the
choral literature written for "equal voices," much of it in three parts, so scored
that two adjacent voices such as alto or tenor may sing the same line, and
so contrived that by transposition it serves equally well the men's, women's,
or mixed chorus.

[2] I hope I shall not be understood as recommending the exclusion of older
persons from choral participation. I believe quite the contrary: that every
human being, however young or old, should be in every way encouraged to
sing with others, and that the opportunities for doing so should be provided.
It is when a conductor is aiming at the highest *artistic* result that I advise the
choice of younger voices.

[3] May I offer an extreme example of this indifference to vocal endowment.
I once had, as members of a chorus, two monotones. It would be impossible
to exaggerate the delight they experienced in having a part in the rehearsal
of great music, and had I denied them one of the real resources of life I
should always have regretted it. They were not in the least sensitive over
their deficiency and made no protest at being seated together a little apart

wearisome to adjust their particular "method" to the needs of tonal homogeneity.[4] They are, besides, prone to object to the amount of rehearsing asked by a conscientious conductor, and their response is, on the whole, less eager than that of the young chorister who is desirous of learning and of pursuing the director's "counsel of perfection."

While a singer's ability to read music is a valuable asset to the conductor, I have never submitted any choral candidate to such a test, nor have I ever discovered that it was necessary to do so. A few readers scattered through the chorus effectually guide the non-readers, and in course of time, and with frequent rehearsal, most singers acquire all the reading skill they need. *Sight* readers — that is, those who can perform the music at sight without mistake — are more often than not a thorn in the conductor's flesh. Their opinion is apt to be that a correct rendering of the notes is the main issue; and since that is accomplished at the first trial, they find the constant repetition of the notes irksome, a fact which the less able readers are not slow to observe. For sight-readers the real romance of rehearsing is an undiscovered country.

In all this I have in mind the conductor whose basic interest in his work is in the revelation to his chorus through experience

---

from the chorus. Fortunately their voices were not strong ones. They sang, without deleterious effect, not less than four major choral works with the Boston Symphony Orchestra and its conductor.

[4] Those who have been trained in the art of solo singing are accustomed to listen to their own voices and to deal with the choral music they sing in the light of their own instructed ideas. On the other hand, I have had in my choruses singers who could perform a solo with all that the soloist's art requires, and immediately thereafter merge their voices in the common choral tone. But he who has struggled with the problems presented by the choral voice that remains inflexibly "solo," that "loves its own singing," as one desperate conductor put it, will sympathize with the visiting director who after leading through a single number a chorus famous for its vocal proficiency, remarked quietly, "Ladies and gentlemen, your singing only emphasizes your innate smallness of mind."

of the beauty and power of great music. Certainly one does not *learn* the *Messiah* by reading the notes at sight, but rather by living with the music until its language and its meaning are unforgettably familiar. That is why, to a conductor, mistakes should never represent time lost; for in correcting those mistakes the music must be sung over again and again, and in that process the music becomes not only the singer's technical property but, what is more important still, his mental and spiritual possession as well. If, however, such considerations do not weigh heavily with either chorus or conductor; if rehearsing, with its attendant benefits, is not the main issue; if it is preparation for a concert or a contest that is the chief and not the incidental object — then, of course, the whole physiognomy of the undertaking is altered. Here, certainly, quick mastery of externals is of the first importance, and to this end sight-readers are an undeniable aid. But when a conductor has as his co-workers a chorus that is young, courageous, pliant, zealous, attentive, corporately intelligent, and interested primarily in the best music and not in the public performance of it, he works under what I should call ideal conditions, and he has only himself to blame if his labors are unproductive.

CHAPTER IV

REHEARSALS

THE MORALE of a chorus, its sense of responsibility, its discipline, bear a definite relation to its artistic achievement; and it is at rehearsals that the total efficiency of the group is established. Slack attendance, lateness, talking while the conductor is giving directions, all these are bound to have their effect upon the singing. It is the conductor who is mainly responsible in these matters; if the music itself is of a quality to command continued enthusiasm in spite of the wear and tear of long practice, and if the rehearsals are events to which the singers eagerly look forward, morale will take care of itself. Conductors sometimes complain that rehearsals cannot compete with social joys such as the theater, bridge, and dancing. Now it is obvious that life is made up of a varied and contrasted set of loyalties, and it is doubtless the better for being so; but the individual must sooner or later and at a definite date choose between conflicting interests. When that time comes he will elect those which afford him the greatest profit from a number of points of view. If he fails to choose, preferring to cultivate a too wide area of activity, then those undertakings which, like choral singing, set regularity of attendance as the first requirement, are bound to suffer heavily. It is the worst possible practice, I believe, as well as an offense against the dignity of the art of music, to plead with singers to attend rehearsals. When in order to maintain the numerical strength of the chorus it seems necessary to do so, questions should first be asked. Is the music what it ought to be? Does the conductor make the rehearsals constantly stimulating? If the answer to these questions is "yes," then the intermittent member should not be made the object of argument, pleading, or probation; he should be refused further connection with the chorus. Such action will be beneficial both to him and to the organization, for he will have more time to pursue other and perhaps equally profitable interests, and the work of the chorus will not be retarded by his mistakes. If an able conductor and estimable music cannot command the almost invariable presence of the singers, then I should unhesitatingly suggest that there be no chorus at all.

I say "the almost invariable presence of the singers," because necessarily there will be an occasional conflict of engagements. No singer should be expected to neglect a domestic or a religious duty in order to attend a rehearsal. The conductor will naturally be solicitous in his attitude, but he must nevertheless decide at what point the singer may be allowed to resume his seat without risk of adversely affecting progress. Under no conditions should a member be allowed to participate in a concert unless he has attended a large majority of the practices. All choral conductors are familiar with the occasional plea, "I broke my leg and haven't been to any rehearsals since the last concert, but my heart will be broken, too, if I don't sing in the performance tomorrow night." Such a request, though it implies commendable enthusiasm, is utterly selfish. In no other sphere of activity where efficiency is put to a crucial trial would it be accepted, and the choral conductor should sympathetically but irrevocably reject it. If the unlucky singer really means what he says, he will be back immediately the concert is over. It is not the blameless absentee who gives the conductor real concern; it is the social will-o'-the-wisp; and that type of singer, once revealed, should be quickly jettisoned.

In determining the number of rehearsals, the conductor must, of course, make up his mind as to whether or not the chorus is to be viewed as just one among many projects. In any case, he will soon discover that, however infrequent rehearsals are, owing to competing engagements, the attendance must be practically and invariably full. Choral practices are sometimes held but once in two weeks, and under such conditions the chorus members are justified in regarding the enterprise as occasional and of no great import. Furthermore, because of the time elapsing between meetings, with consequent and necessary repetitions on the conductor's part, it is doubtful whether any really consistent progress can be made. One rehearsal a week is the generally accepted practice, but where enthusiasm runs high two and even three rehearsals may be held. In such cases a rehearsal of one hour to an hour and a half, without a rest period, is sufficient. If the conductor keeps the interest at white heat the intermission becomes an artificial and resented interruption. A wise and able conductor never wearies his chorus either physically or mentally; he does quite the reverse.

An amphitheater with rising tiers of seats is most favorable as a rehearsal room. Under these conditions a conductor may hear all parts of the chorus equally well. Where the room is long and narrow, each part should be assigned to the front seats at successive rehearsals in order that its work may be adequately checked by the director. A haphazard seating of the chorus is not advisable. Seating lists facilitate the taking of attendance, and morale is improved by the constant association of the same group of singers. In the seating by parts and by individuals, care should be taken in the first case to acquire the proper balance and in the second not to permit one or two voices to disturb the homogeneity of tone. The handling of individual voices is one of the most delicate of the conductor's tasks. Inevitably, he will have at his disposal singers who represent in varying degree the virtues for which he strives at rehearsal. Singers possessing loud and (or) trained voices usually expect to occupy the front seats, an anticipation which the conductor is bound tactfully to disappoint. If he does not do so, the effect will be of a few "principals" with an accompanying group of partially audible co-participators. The problem of the most painless way of locating the "best" voices toward the rear is a perennial and vexing one, and the conductor will often have to deal with each case individually. The vanity of singers is common knowledge, and it must be regarded even if it cannot be respected. Generally it will not do simply to assign a good voice to a rear seat. It must be explained to the singer that, although his voice is beautiful and his musical presence indispensable, his value to the less gifted members is materially diminished by his position in the front row. The chorus rely on him, they need to feel behind them the reinforcement and confidence that his superior vocal equipment and trained musicianship afford, etc., etc., all depending on the conductor's adroitness in discovering the weak spot in the particular armor of pride he is trying to pierce. I do not in the least suggest that there is only guile in this practice. The reasons given are true reasons, and they must, in the common interest, be respected by the singer to whom they are offered. At the same time they must be presented tactfully and with the complete sincerity they deserve.

In cases where there is a reasonable equality in numbers or volume among the four parts, the customary grouping is, I believe, as represented in Example 11 (page 34), though the conductor may, if he chooses, reverse the relative positions of the soprano-tenor and alto-bass "families."

A particular problem in seating arises when one or two parts are deficient in strength or numbers. In American choruses it is usually tenors and basses that are scarce, and in such instances a pyramidal type of seating is often helpful.

By putting, say, one or two tenors and basses with inconspicuous and blending voices in the front row with the others of their respective parts directly behind them, as shown in Example 12, the conductor is assured that the men's voices will be adequately heard without the necessity of "over-singing."

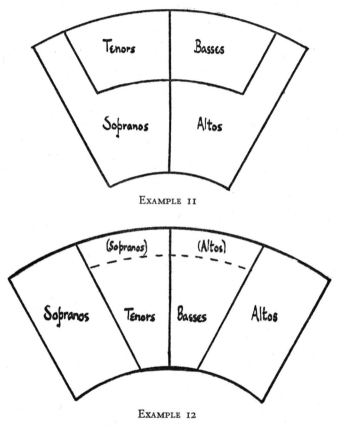

EXAMPLE 11

EXAMPLE 12

At concerts the seating arrangements which are followed at rehearsals should be preserved as nearly as possible, and on all occasions the conductor should stand sufficiently distant from the chorus to enable the total sound to focus on him as a center.

The conductor will, of course, study his program with care, and will plan as far as he can the treatment of each piece. But he must do more than this; he must be so familiar with the music that he need not glance at it save as an occasional aid to memory. The conductor who hunches himself over his score and gazes fixedly at the page as though he had never seen it before works under an insurmountable handicap. In the first place the chorus will resentfully suspect that he doesn't know his music and will see no reason why, if he never looks at them, they should look at him. Besides, any preoccupation with the printed page prevents the conductor from employing one of his mightiest weapons, namely facial expression. The impassivity of the Anglo-Saxon countenance is proverbial, and it accounts for a good deal of the wooden choral singing we hear. One could hardly assess the value to the conductor of a mobile and expressive face, nor enumerate the variety of meanings it can convey to the chorus. Hands may give mechanical directions and may even assume an interpretative function, but it is primarily through facial expression in conjunction with gesture that the conductor imparts those details which are supplementary to technical drill. Thus he conveys his satisfaction, which gives encouragement, or his displeasure, which stimulates to greater effort. The singers know from his glance the emotions which the text and music arouse in him, and they try to make those emotions articulate. Though he never sings with the chorus, because the sound of his own voice would prevent his hearing the chorus and thus render him helpless to correct or admonish, he often soundlessly forms the words. This practice, added to gesture and facial expression, puts at the conductor's command the most eloquent means of communication imaginable. And when, as will happen, he finds himself so deeply moved after the performance of some piece — so moved by the beauty of the music, the superlative quality of the performance, and the consciousness that he has had a part in working this miracle — that he dare not for a moment turn about to acknowledge the applause lest he betray to the audience his state of mind, then he may realize the true value of an expressive countenance, for it is only by such means that he is able to offer to his singers a tribute deeper than ever words could pay and that he can make them understand that he has shared with them a rare and memorable experience. It is for the conductor to act out in a quiet way with hands and face every implication of text and music. He need not fear appearing grotesque in the eyes of the chorus; but far better that he should appear so than that he should resemble, as many a conductor does, an indifferent or unwilling victim caught in the net of unavoidable circumstance.

If the conductor does not watch his chorus he cannot know, of course, whether or not the singers are watching him, and one of the first mechanical details of choral training is insistence on looking at the conductor. In the earlier rehearsals or with a new piece some allowance may be made, but as soon as possible the chorus should be expected to glance rapidly back and forth from conductor to music. Singers will follow with evident concern the progress of the notes to the very last dot on the page (thereby missing the first measure on the next page) as though they expected the symbols to play tricks by converting themselves into something else. I have sometimes pointed out that much less harm would be done by a singer not sufficiently versatile to read his music and at the same time follow the conductor if he would give over singing entirely and fasten his attention on the beat. In what appear to be hopeless cases the conductor is sometimes tempted to escape the dilemma by stamping or clapping his hands in time with the music. No more fatal method of encouraging the chorus to ignore the conductor could be employed. Obviously these methods cannot be used in public performance, and it is courting disaster to employ them in rehearsal. By the same token, a singer's keeping time (his own, but not necessarily the conductor's) by foot-tapping should be forbidden.

Any varied program will contain both accompanied and unaccompanied music. Too many programs, unfortunately, are overburdened with music requiring instrumental support. This is sometimes due to the conductor's fear that for one reason or another his chorus is not sufficiently skillful to be trusted in *a cappella* music; but, regardless of type, practically every piece should be rehearsed without accompaniment if for no other purpose than to encourage self-reliance. There is a large and diverse *a cappella* literature, and the highest virtues of choral singing are best displayed by means of it. No conductor, certainly, should neglect to offer his singers the enjoyment of this rich segment of the composer's art. Sometimes it is fear that a chorus will flat that deters the director from selecting unaccompanied music. For my own part, I believe that the ideal of a correctly maintained pitch in *a cappella* singing is overemphasized. It is, perhaps, a by-product of our respect for instrumental accuracy. Naturally, one holds that ideal constantly before the chorus and expresses proper gratification when it is realized, but, provided the singing is in other respects satisfactory, a moderate departure from true pitch is not catastrophic when all four parts change practically simultaneously, not too suddenly, and in the same proportion, and when the basses are not crowded down to an inaudible depth. Comparatively few singers have an unerring sense of pitch, but frequent reference to the pitch as given by the piano, plus the admonition to "think high" and to breathe freely and often, will go far toward making a chorus proficient in preserving the original key. The acoustics of a room or the composer's ineptitude are often to blame for pitch variations; and some pieces, for no determinable cause, will refuse, even when sung by an expert chorus, to sound tonally secure. All else failing, a practically infallible cure is afforded by raising (or sometimes lowering) the given pitch a half or a whole tone. If that is done, the piece will in most cases remain fixed at its proper pitch.

Inability to hold the pitch is sometimes due to fatigue resulting from unskillful rehearsing. Too long practices are not nearly so harmful as badly conducted ones, and the director should exhaust every means to lighten the tasks of the singers. A long continued forte, for example, is as taxing as it is unnecessary. All technical ends may be satisfactorily met by frequently rehearsing mezzo-forte, or even piano, a piece which, in performance, will be sung fortissimo. In the same way sustained high passages are less wearisome if they are rehearsed an octave lower. Among numerous ill-chosen methods which tend to make a rehearsal irksome is that of concentration on the notes of one or two parts while the rest of the chorus is left idle. Some rehearsing of individual parts is bound to be done, especially when notes are being learned, but such rehearsing ought to be distributed as evenly as possible among the four parts, and in no case should a majority of the chorus be left silent for an appreciable time.

Sustained interest at rehearsals depends not a little on the order in which the pieces are taken up. No prearranged scheme is likely to be strictly adhered to, but the principle of alternating styles, loud and soft, vigorous and gentle, fast and slow, is fundamentally sound; and the initial piece should by all means be calculated to enlist the immediate interest of the chorus. To begin with a dirge is always unwise and sometimes prophetic.

But of all offenses against the patience of the chorus, against efficient rehearsing, and, it might almost be said, against music itself, the worst is that sin committed by us all, the sin of *talking too much*. Clearly, a chorus attends practice because it wants to sing, not because it wishes to be lectured to; yet many conductors seem unable to stem the rhetorical Niagaras that burst forth on any provocation. Indeed a conductor who finds it difficult to cover the required ground in rehearsal ought not to blame that difficulty on the backwardness of his chorus until he has assured himself that he has not indulged his tongue too generously.[1]

Constant interruption of the singing, with its almost inevitable accompaniment of explanation, results in serious loss of time and exasperation on the part of the chorus. If one teaches principles rather than cases he will make unnecessary these frequent breaks in the continuity of the rehearsal. For example, if you want every final consonant to be heard, state this, at the first opportunity, as a principle to be constantly adhered to and explain why you establish it. In the beginning it may be necessary to rehearse a passage in which every fault except the omission of final consonants is ignored. Little by little, however, the observance of this principle will become practically automatic, and only occasional reference to it need be made. If, on the other hand, you deal with each final consonant as a separate technical incident, the chorus will so view it and will require constant prodding on that point. Interruptions of the singing for technical correction may often be avoided by shouted exhortations to give attention to some impending detail the failure to observe which will prompt the conductor to stop the rehearsal and dilate on the offense.

The truth is that, in a large majority of cases, language fails entirely to clarify the conductor's wishes on technical matters. But there is a means of communication which is illuminating as well as time-saving, and it embodies a precept of workman-

---

[1] I once had a student of conducting who was an incorrigible talker, but he always insisted that he had talked no more than was needed to make clear his ideas to the chorus. Without letting it be known, I asked a stenographer to attend a rehearsal and take down all that this particular student said during his allotted time. To his surprise and humiliation he was forced, when he had taken his seat, to hear his own words repeated. What he had said made up a futile hodgepodge of unrelated, uninstructive, and badly expressed ideas. Eight minutes had been spent in singing, twelve in talking.

ship which, more than any other, I would urge on the young conductor: *sing whenever you feel the inclination to talk*. Sing one passage only, and you will have accomplished at least three objectives. First, you will have furnished the chorus with a vital example not only of how you wish those particular measures to be sung, but of your technical ideal for *all* choral music similar to the section under consideration. Your example will be, in fact, a very brief wordless lecture on phrasing, tone, breathing, interpretation, and pronunciation. Second, you will not fail to reveal the emotion which the music generates in you, and, if your illustration is an eloquent one, you may be fortunate enough to find that it was contagious. And lastly, you will have saved time; as to how important that achievement is any seasoned conductor will testify, for the director's most difficult problem is that of accomplishing all that he has to do in his few hours of rehearsal. These are measurable benefits, but if their full value is to be realized, you must reinforce them in the following way: when you have finished your example, simply ask the chorus to repeat the same passage, and let them sing it immediately. By no means allow the effect of your illustration to grow cold. If the singers return to you a reasonably faithful copy of the model you have supplied them, you will have fulfilled the choral conductor's first function, that of teacher, not lecturer.[2]

The urge to expound will sometimes prompt oratorical excursions into the beauty or significance of the material, perhaps with the idea that the music is "over the heads" of the chorus and that your protestations will make it more palatable. Im-

[2] A quick method of correction consists in imitating the bad singing of the chorus. This is, however, a dangerous expedient unless it is employed with the utmost tact and never with a suspicion of bitterness or ridicule. Parodies of this kind should appear to be offered with humorous and not with didactic intent, and the conductor should be the first to laugh. Then should come the conductor's own example of correct singing, followed immediately, of course, by the chorus's response.

plied apologies of this sort are a pure waste of time, for converts to a high aesthetic standard are not won by fine words; if the music is beautiful it will state its own claims to acceptance far more effectively than you can set them forth. You can waste time, too, and injure morale by constant praise; frequent commendation dulls the edge of discriminating and especially deserved congratulation; but when the occasion arises, a single glance of gratitude and admiration will convey far more than verbal enconiums. The foregoing admonition — and I fear this paragraph is heavy with negative advice — will seem merely rhetorical to those conductors who, cursed with a sluggish or inattentive chorus, would seize almost hysterically upon any plausible excuse for lauding their singers. But these conductors should remember *per contra* that consistent scolding will yield a state of dull discouragement more damaging than that lethargy of self-satisfaction which is induced by overpraise.[3]

While either commendation or reproof may be employed unwisely, the unforgivable sin of conducting, so serious that it has damaged more than one conductor's prestige and in some cases has resulted in termination of tenure, is the losing of one's temper. A conductor may be distressed at the inability of his chorus to realize his wishes, but he must nevertheless remain cheerful and encouraging. He may be justifiably wrathy, and expressively so, at inattention and carelessness; but beyond that he should not go. The singers must respect not only the musician but the man as well, and a single loss of temper may jeopardize relations between chorus and director, a situation which can never yield the best artistic results.

[3] Many years ago, during a rehearsal at which I had distinguished myself mainly by a variety and magnitude of excoriating comment, the singers closed their books one by one. When I asked the cause of this, a member of the chorus said that it had occurred to him that it would be easier if all remained silent, since the singing was in my evident opinion bad beyond redemption. I hope I have never since been guilty of nagging.

A too frequent recourse to words in various connections is not, however, the only destructive and time-wasting pit into which the conductor may fall. Some directors place considerable dependence on extra-musical detail, such as the costuming of the singers or the execution of figures on the platform. Others cultivate theatrical methods of singing or extreme interpretations of the music. These methods are usually employed by traveling choruses or organizations which are the objects of a pilgrimage, and they originate in the fear that the customer will expect more than music for his money. In view of the disheartening apathy of the American public toward choral music one finds it difficult to quarrel with this attitude, but of the two types of sensationalism, the purely entertaining and amusing and the artistically debased, the latter, at least, may be unqualifiedly condemned. Belonging to neither type, but definitely in the class of the mystifying and "how-do-they-do-it" devices, is the starting of each piece without the prompting of a pitch audible to the listeners. The concert-goer so sensitive that he is shocked by a preliminary pitch sounded on pianoforte or organ is to be pitied and ignored; and a conductor who thinks that his chorus is a better one because it can dispense with a safe precaution against disaster is mistaken. Beginning without audible pitch is a "stunt," the mastery of which involves much time that might better be spent in at least two ways: first in improving the singing, and second in enlarging the repertoire.

I have already suggested in this chapter that the prime function of the conductor is that of teacher. But the art of teaching includes much more than the mere exposition of facts. In every subject there is hidden somewhere an imaginative element which may make the pursuit of that subject an adventure. If it is to be so, it will be the enthusiasm of the teacher and his perception of the imaginative possibilities of the material which will bring this about. Now the imaginative factor, while it is not the whole of either music teaching or learning, is certainly a major item, and it is the almost complete absence of imagination, with a corresponding glorification of the mechanics of pedagogy and an indifference to the quality of subject matter, that has been the scourge of American music teaching. Let it be said, then, that however relentlessly the conductor may insist on the technical excellence of the singing, drill must never be an end in itself. The chorus must be made to feel that the sole justification for technique is that it makes possible the final and full revelation of the beauty that resides in the music. Furthermore, a conductor who is not persuaded of the artistic validity of the subject matter (in this case music) cannot teach it to a chorus with sincerity and enthusiasm, without which nothing really fine can be achieved. I would strongly advise, therefore, that any musician who is in a position to do so, and who possesses profound convictions as to good and bad in musical literature, should refuse the post of conductor under conditions which deny him sole responsibility for the selection of the material to be sung. It would, I know, be difficult to persuade most people that there is an artistic as well as a moral conscience, and that for the musician of sensitive taste an offense against the first may well be more distressing even than a departure from right behavior. It is so, nonetheless, and there are numbers of choral conductors in this country who are as bitterly conscious of the dishonesty of their position as a Mohammedan forced to preach the doctrine of transubstantiation.

To the conductor, concerts may well be no more than exciting interruptions of the processes by which the powers of his chorus are developed. It is at rehearsals that the real work is done. There the conductor learns the capacities of his singers, develops those capacities by ingenuity and persuasiveness, and establishes one half of a reciprocating relationship out of which may grow the final realization of his musical ideals. There the chorus, not on parade, grows into a corporate artistic individuality, stands on terms of real intimacy with the music, penetrates into its true significance, and learns how to make the composer's message eloquent and moving. Indeed, for the singers, too, as well as for the conductor, I am sure it is the rehearsal and not the concert that most often spells adventure.

CHAPTER V

CHORAL TECHNIQUE

IT WOULD not be possible to include within one volume all the technical minutiae which go to make up chorus training. The conductor, once he has set up for himself a standard of performance, will employ those devices which lead most quickly and effectively to the realization of that ideal, but he will employ those devices flexibly and with discrimination. There is perhaps no single precept, except that of a precise attack and release, which, in spite of a conductor's convictions regarding its soundness, will not sooner or later be modified by the demands of a particular musical situation. Take the portamento, for example. Slurring between notes is a common failing of the untutored singer, and a conductor might state with comparative assurance that it is never to be countenanced. Yet choral music, which is technically akin to string music, sometimes, though rarely, requires a suggestion of portamento, as in Example 13 (page 46), and neglect to ask for it may lessen the effectiveness of a vocal line and rob the music of some of its virtue.[1] Example 14 (page 47), however, is representative of cases in which the unfortunate combination of certain syllables and notes seems to invite slurring of a most disagreeable sort. Here the portamento is particularly hard to avoid because of the high vocal writing. But, regardless of range, wherever in the course of a composition this or a similarly ungrateful union of text and music occurs, the best and easiest solution is the taking of a very short catch-breath.

[1] The pernicious practice of scooping (attacking just under the pitch of the note) is, of course, invariably to be forbidden.

EXAMPLE 13

Not alone the musical situation of the moment but the size of the chorus as well will condition the technique. Exaggerations which are necessary in the case of a large group may be modified where the chorus is a small one.[2]

EXAMPLE 14

There are seven cardinal issues to be met: Pronunciation, Tone, Breathing, Phrasing, Rhythm, Variety in Dynamics, and Impressiveness. These are the whole of which an infinity of detail is the parts. Interpretation is not the chorus's business; it is the conductor's; and when the chorus understands how the conductor wishes the piece to be *interpreted*, that understanding is conveyed by the chorus in terms of *impressiveness*. Impressiveness is in great measure the sum of the other six details; these, however, must be dealt with as principles, though the mastering of them may be made less arduous by telescoping. Thus the conductor sings a passage in which several principles are exemplified. In their first response the chorus will not observe all of them, but repeated illustrations with a word of explanation as to what is lacking will eventually bring about the desired result, and more and more it will be pronunciation that the conductor will dwell upon.

[2] The choice of repertoire, too, is bound to be affected by numerical strength. A choir of two hundred can no more achieve delicacy in a madrigal than a chorus of twenty can proclaim the thunders of a Handelian chorus.

Pronunciation

Pronunciation is the key to impressive choral singing, the root from which all choral virtues spring. It is, nonetheless, one of the weakest departments of choral work. Conductors strive honestly to produce it, but generally they are satisfied that "clear" pronunciation is either adequate or all that is possible. By "clear" pronunciation I refer to the more or less careful articulation of each word by every singer. "Colloquial" pronunciation, or the conversational treatment of language, is as indefensible in choral singing as it is common.[3] An absolutely intelligible and impressive rendering of the text is obtained only by "meticulous" pronunciation which involves the singer in frank exaggerations. Too much choral pronunciation copies the methods of solo singing, though it should be obvious that, while a word as uttered by one singer may be precisely clear, that word may become quite unintelligible when pronounced simultaneously and in the same manner by one hundred singers.[4]

Consistently intelligible pronunciation is of the first importance because without it the listener has no clue to the animating source of the music. The composer's music is what it is because the words suggested it. An escape from the dilemma imposed on singers and hearers alike is sometimes offered by printing

---

[3] A short time ago I heard a Finnish chorus introduce into its program a piece sung in English. Realizing that the singers could have but a general idea of the meaning of the text, I was astonished at the impressiveness of the performance. The explanation was, of course, that the difficulty of singing in a foreign tongue had made it necessary to learn the exact pronunciation of each word; and this, consummated by the most painstaking articulation, resulted in an effectiveness that was almost dramatic. I had many times heard that same selection sung by English-speaking choruses, but never with such significance.

[4] Many soloists place almost exclusive reliance on beautiful tone. How vivid language accompanied by music may be is amply demonstrated in the singing of John McCormack.

the text on the program. In such cases the singer may feel himself relieved of the obligation to be lucid, and the hearer need not strain his ears in an effort to find out what the singing is about. How the composer would feel is another matter. I venture to think that he would prefer that the listeners should give their undivided attention to the singers, the living medium for his ideas as represented in the wedding of music and words, rather than that they should concentrate on a printed page which is a lifeless record of material which constitutes but a part of the whole.

The impression I receive from a good deal of choral singing is that conductors lay almost exclusive emphasis on vowels. As a matter of fact, it is consonants that are of overwhelming importance. Once a tonal method has been established, the vowels will, save for occasional special treatment, take care of themselves. Without consonants, however, the whole fabric of the music becomes flabby and meaningless. If the word "cold" is to sound cold, it is not alone the coloring of the vowel, but also the distinctness with which the c, l, and d are brought out that will make it so. If the word "bright" is to suggest its meaning the b, r, and t must literally shine. The letter r should almost always be rolled; less often, perhaps, in the case of the final r, but even then it must be clearly heard, especially if the sense of the word is in some degree dramatic.

> There, O there! O there! where'er I go
> I leave my heart behind me.

Although singers may pronounce the r with care, unless that letter is rolled it invariably gives the effect of w, especially if the chorus is sizeable. This accounts for the constant choral phenomenon which results in the sound of a word flatly denying its meaning. Such a word is "strong," which suggests only weakness when it is heard as "stwong."

The letter h is the work-horse among consonants. It possesses a great deal of importance in its own right, and it may further be used as a reinforcement in the overcoming of certain difficulties. Unless the slightly percussive quality of the *h* is utilized, such words as "holy," "host," and "happy" not only lose something of their significance, but they fail, as well, to

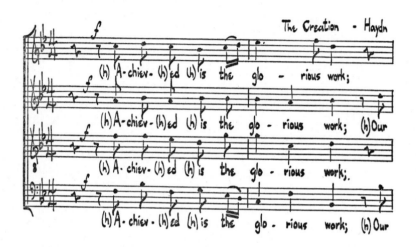

EXAMPLE 15

contribute their necessary share to the rhythmical flow of the music. Another salutary use of the letter as an aid to clarity, rhythm, and clean-cut attack consists in placing the *h* before the initial vowel of any word. All conductors know the difficulty of avoiding what is called, I believe, a glottis attack when the opening word begins with a vowel or when there is reason to stress a word in the middle of a phrase. Two instances are given in Example 15 (page 50).

If the attack is forte the difficulty is less great, though the *h* materially strengthens the impact; but where the beginning is pianissimo as, perhaps, in *Adoramus,* the following method will make a ragged attack less audible: the chorus, as always, will breathe *in* with your warning-beat; as your hand begins the indication of the singing-beat the chorus breathes out soundlessly on the letter *h*; and as you reach the customary point in your motion where the attack is to occur, the singers slide gently from the *h* into the vowel sound.

The enervating effect of a slurred interval, especially a wide one, is easily avoided by the repetition of the vowel or diphthong on the second of the two notes with the accompaniment of the ever-useful *h*. Thus:

EXAMPLE 16

The letter *h* is most valuable, however, when it is introduced between two adjacent vowels; and the common neglect of this device leads, first, to rhythmlessness and, second, to unintelligibility and an occasional effect of word-scrambling suggestive of James Joyce's later prose style. "Dowopen" (do open), "myyeye" (my eye), and "whowis" (who is) both look and sound confusing. If, however, they are sung "do (h)open," "my (h)eye," and "who (h)is," their meaning is instantly clear.

Now one may object that "do (h)open" is quite as obscure as "dowopen"; and, on the face of it, this would appear to be true. As the device of the interpolated *h* is the first among a number of "mechanical" methods which I have to recommend, I should like at this time to deal with all its implications as representative of my profound belief in artificial means as aids to artistic choral singing.

The problem in this particular case is to escape the scourge of unrhythmical singing and senseless text-delivery. The obvious and natural antidote for "dowopen" is to ask the singers simply to pronounce the two *o*'s carefully, not allowing them to run together. In the beginning of his career probably every conductor has tried that cure, and, if he has, he has found it unavailing. The difficulty is both a physical and a mental one. In conversation the singer has said "dowopen" and has been immediately understood; whereas when you explain to him that such pronunciation is inadmissible in singing because what is understandable when spoken by one individual is quite meaningless when sung by a hundred, and that he must distinguish clearly between the two *o*'s, either he emphasizes each one without succeeding in eliminating the intervening *w* (dOwOpen) or the effort to keep the *o*'s apart without employing some artificial wedge is so laborious that even if he doesn't mentally curse it as a bit of needless preciosity, the constantly painful repetition of it will eventually cause him to lapse once more into his natural conversational usage. Yet, if the singing of a chorus is to be first-rate, this requirement of articulated consecutive vowels must be unequivocally met; and the answer is to be found in some device which is so patently artificial and so free of physical effort that it will in time become second nature.[5] Such a device is the interpolated *h*. Among many and conscientious efforts to win a departure from the fatal colloquial merging of two successive vowels, this is the only one I have ever found to be successful.[6]

In order to allay any fears regarding the final effectiveness of this method, let me recount my own invariable experience of it. Like any device of the sort, it wars with habit; but once the chorus understands its purpose and has practiced its use, it becomes instinctive, first because it involves a simple operation of everyday speech as when one says, "How [not 'ow] do you do?" and second because the singers quickly discover how greatly it vitalizes the whole effect of the music. It is, of course, machinery; it must be insisted on as machinery, and for some time at rehearsals it will be audible as machinery. If it continued to be so, the time spent on it would have been wasted. But two things never fail to happen with this as with other such means: first, some chorus members either cannot or will not do what you ask, a condition which balances overemphasis on the part of others; and second, before long the singers, realizing what you are really aiming at, bring their common sense into play and gradually modify the application of the device until the machinery disappears, leaving to be heard only incisively articulated vowels.[7]

[5] It is, perhaps, a significant indication of a casual attitude toward proficiency in choral singing that many a man who spends hours in the hot sun learning to "follow through" with his driver, or in mastering the intricacies of tennis "form," resents the suggestion that choral art demands more of him than a lusty voice and familiarity with the English language.

[6] Another valuable use of the interpolated *h* is in the performing of the comparatively rapid roulades common to eighteenth-century music, where clarity and evenness are always difficult to attain.

[7] When singers have been slow in applying mechanical aids or have appeared to resent what seemed to them a futile and laborious discipline, I have asked the more experienced members, those who have had a year or more of practice,

Standing high among the conductor's torments is the letter *s*. Some singers, owing, perhaps, to dental malformation, seem to wring from this letter the ultimate in unmusical sound. These singers should be urged to lisp or even omit their *s*'s entirely. Occasionally, however, some text will require a particularly sibilant treatment. Take the following example from Brahms' *Liebeslieder*:

> Nein es ist nicht auszukommen mit den Leuten;
> Alles wissen sie so giftig auszudeuten!
> Bin ich heiter, hegen soll ich lose Triebe;
> Bin ich still, so heisst's ich wäre irr' aus liebe!

> (No, there is no bearing with these spiteful neighbors;
> All one dost interpret wrongly, each one labours!
> Am I merry? Then by evil thoughts I'm haunted;
> Am I sad? They say I am with love demented!)

The best practice in dealing with *s*, as with other consonants, is to attach the letter to the second of two syllables even when it belongs with the first. "Ma-ster" not "mas-ter"; "fa-ster" not "fas-ter." If this is not done the chorus will "scatter" the *s*, as "mas-s-s-ter," or will come to it immediately and continue to hiss until the second syllable is taken, as "masss-ter." In the case of an initial *s* followed by a vowel, the chorus should be urged to pass to the vowel as quickly as possible. Final *s*'s can only become precise after much practice by the chorus and through very definite indications on the conductor's part. The sounds *sh* and *ch* are generally treated in much the same manner as is *s*. Let me say again, however, that circumstances condition method. For example, one would not sing the words "such as" "su-chas" because then the sense would be obscured;

---

to sing a certain passage as a model for the new members. The singing proves the reasonableness of my requests and demonstrates, at the same time, the complete absence of artificial technical devices from the finished performance, a fact which never fails to impress the beginners deeply.

in that case the solution would be "such (h)as"; and no singer having consideration for the sensibilities of the public will need prompting in the pronunciation of "his will."

Where two *s*'s occur together, one may be omitted; and it is generally the second of the two that is sounded. "Creatures share" may be sung "creature share," "his soul" as "hi soul," etc.

A deep-rooted fault, so common among chorus singers that it might almost be called the "original sin" of amateur vocalists, is "closing in" on consonants. This is sometimes due to an indecisive beat, the chorus not being certain when to change from one syllable to the next, but even the best conductors find it a serious factor to be reckoned with. Take, for instance, the word "element." The average singer will hurry from the *e* to the *l*, thence to the *m*, and finally to the *nt*. The result is that he has "sung" mainly the consonants, whereas it is, of course, the vowels which sustain the tone. Such a transfer of the singing function to consonants only ends in complete vocal frustration. In situations where brilliance and volume are required it is sometimes permissible to omit a consonant entirely lest it destroy the effect of the vowel. In Example 17 (page 56) everything depends on the sustaining of the *a* in "sancto." If the *nc* is sung it is bound to steal valuable tone from the *a*, particularly as the whole passage moves quickly. The *nc* may, therefore, be justifiably omitted.

Now it must be understood that if this were the only passage where the word "sancto" occurred the foregoing recommendation would not be valid, because, above all else, the *sense* of the text must be made clear. But the word "sancto" has been heard in this chorus again and again in connection with its surrounding text, so that failure to pronounce these two letters is not going to confuse the listener. Furthermore, Bach has supplied at this point such an exciting accompaniment that no one is likely to discover the omission of the two consonants. (At least no one ever has, so far as I know.)

EXAMPLE 17

Pronunciation is materially affected by the style of the music and also by the tempo. A contrapuntal piece demands a great measure of care with the text, as the various syllables of a word are unlikely to occur simultaneously in all parts. And where the speed is excessive, comprehension of the text is well-nigh impossible. The tendency of some conductors to whip up a choral allegro to a presto originates, I suspect, in the desire to produce the kind of stimulation that grows out of sheer orchestral speed. Like most other attempts to transfer to the chorus what is, by nature, instrumental, an unduly fast tempo only defeats the composer's purpose. When one aims at the expression of ideas that are best conveyed at high speed, he commits those ideas to an instrument; but when he sets a text to music, the first requirement he makes is that that text, without which the music is comparatively meaningless, shall be heard and understood.

TONE

At the first rehearsal the conductor discovers that there are almost as many varieties of tone-production in his chorus as there are singers. Some amateurs, indeed, appear to refute the

the most diverse and sensitive coloring and of being bent in or out to characterize any textual requirement.[8] Subjective tone, furthermore, guarantees the destruction of individual idiosyncrasies of tone production and yields one magnified choral voice as no other tone can. That voice is not beautiful in the sense that a *solo* voice may be beautiful; but there is, as I have said before, no time for individual voice lessons in the schedule of the average chorus, even were such instruction desirable. I have sometimes referred to subjective tone as "distinguished mediocrity" in the sense that the separate voices which form it are often mediocre and assume distinction only when merged into homogeneity under one method. Such a flexible and versatile tone when supported by other details of technique furnishes, for me at least, the ideal medium. Subjective tone, like clear pronunciation, is won only by insistence on a certain amount of artificial method. Thus the word "Gloria" in the earlier stages of the discipline will sound like "glowr-r-(u)i-aw," but once the principle is understood and the quality of the desired tone is in the singers' ears, the chorus will make the inevitable modifications and the word will be pronounced normally, but with a full and pervading roundness.

Composers sometimes destroy the best effect of their music by unskillful manipulation of the text, and conductors are occasionally tempted to put the matter right by substitution. Humming is one of the most common escapes, but it should never be employed when the words are essential to the musical meaning. To hum the text of a Bach chorale, for example, is indefensible. Where humming is indicated by the composer or is extensively employed in the course of a single program, every effort should be made to gain tonal variety by employing differ-

[8] A newspaper once published a picture of the Harvard Glee Club singing out-of-doors. As a football coach could, under parallel circumstances, tell whether the players were carrying out their assignments properly, so I could determine whether the facial "setting" for tone was in each case correct.

ent vowels. On the whole, the most monotonous, mechanical, and often quite ineffective humming is that done with closed lips. It tends to be nasal, especially when "pushed" and is not a very good conveyance for significant melodic lines. As a contrast to it, humming with open lips using one or another of the vowel sounds (particularly *oo*) is valuable. Another irksome detail consists in the composer's occasionally calling for sounds like *e* as in "met," *ee* as in "feel," *i* as in "tip," to be sung forte on very high tones or, under any dynamic conditions, on very low notes. In such circumstances it is advisable, provided the sense of the passage has been established, to replace the troublesome sound by *ah*, which allows the singers freedom and reasonable sonority.

Breathing

The conductor need not be disturbed if, in the early stages of chorus training, the tone is frequently interrupted. It is mainly, but not entirely, the interpolated *h* and the meticulous pronunciation of consonants that will be responsible for this. Now except for deliberate phrasing the tone should not, of course, be broken, and occasional admonitions to avoid "choppy" singing and to take longer and more frequent breaths will rectify this trouble. If, say, the words "(h)I have (h)all" are sung with one continuous and smooth-flowing breath, the articulation will be perfectly clear and the tone cannot possibly be interrupted. Almost from the beginning the conductor should insist on breath-control; not in the scientific sense in which singing teachers use those words, but as meaning that the singer must at all times have plenty of breath on hand. In other words, no attempt should be made to perform a long phrase under one breath as a soloist must do; instead catch-breaths must be taken whenever there is danger of the supply running short. Even at the risk of being tiresome the conductor should din into the ears of his chorus the maxim, "Breathe naturally, deeply,

and often." [9] Where, as in the finale to Beethoven's Ninth
Symphony, the chorus is asked to hold a single note so long
that one breath will not suffice, the singers may be instructed
to breathe at will, each time letting themselves in fairly softly
on the vowel with a rapid crescendo to the required dynamic.
If the chorus is comparatively small the breathing may be de-
liberately "staggered" in something like the following manner:
those whose last names begin with the letter A through G will
breathe at one point, H through M and N through Z breathing
respectively at selected spots shortly thereafter. An interesting
example of "staggered" breathing is the unison passage for
basses in the "Et resurrexit" of the B minor Mass, where, owing
to the sudden octave skip, there is no time for breath. By allowing only the second basses to sing the passage "mortuos," the
first basses have time to prepare for the attack on *ju* of "judi-
care." This, through the word "vivos," they may sing alone,
being rejoined by the second basses for the final passage "et
mortuos." (See Example 18.)

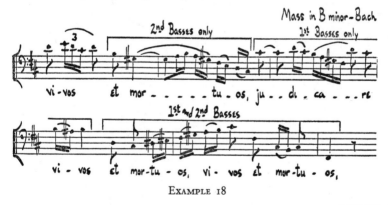

EXAMPLE 18

[9] For an example of complete indifference to human lung capacity the
reader is referred to the final pages of the last of Ravel's *Trois Chansons*.
Only singers adept in the art of catch-breathing will be able to perform this
very effective chorus without flatting or disregarding the composer's directions as to tempo and dynamics.

In choral music as in congregational hymns there are obviously convenient breathing spots which, if taken advantage of, destroy the flow of the music and the meaning of the text. Under these circumstances the chorus must be directed to breathe at some previous and perhaps illogical point (though not all the singers at the same point) in order that the necessary integration may not be broken. Ornate choral style such as that common to eighteenth-century music requires the utmost attention to breathing. No ordinary singer can complete impressively a sixteen-measure roulade on *a* of "Alleluia" unless he keeps his lungs full of air practically throughout the process; and if he continues too long without replenishing there will be gaps in the music and sudden decrescendos in the volume. If the chorus is a moderately large one (and it probably will be if it is performing music of this type), the continuous breath-taking by the chorus will not be noticed because in all probability not more than two or three singers will breathe at the same time. Where long roulades occur, a guarantee of continuity consists in the chorus generally taking breath in the middle of a group of four sixteenth-notes, let us say, rather than at the beginning of the group, thus avoiding unnatural accentuation. The truth is that most roulades of this kind must gain in volume up to the last note, a condition which is im-

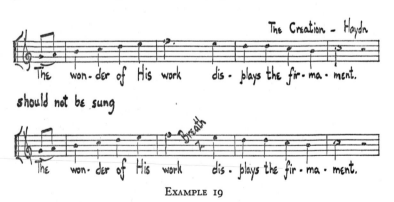

EXAMPLE 19

possible unless frequent breathing takes place.[10] Illogical gaps in the singing are also caused by the stealing of a beat in order to replenish breath. Every singer should be taught that in a measure of 4/4 time, for example, a dotted half-note does not end with the beginning of the third beat, but with the beginning of the fourth. Thus in Example 19 a breath after "work" destroys the sense of the passage and will generally result in slighting the two all-important consonants k and d. If a breath is necessary at that point it should be, at most, the briefest of catch-breaths.

It is hardly necessary to say that the requirement of sustained tone on held notes is a fundamental one. Too often a chord which should remain fortissimo to the end is allowed to diminish because the singers lack sufficient breath; and sustained pianissimo chords, especially final ones, sometimes evaporate for the same reason. There are few experiences more humiliating to the conductor than to find himself holding a closing chord while one part after another collapses breathless. This detail may well be dealt with separately at rehearsals. Singers should be practiced in the use of catch-breaths and of insinuating themselves gently again and again into the choral texture; and it should be made quite clear that no one is to stop singing — even if he has to take twenty breaths — until the conductor gives the cut-off sign. Normal long breathing must be cultivated as a foundation, but a powerful ally is a device already referred to, namely, the catch-breath. Provided the singer in breathing never allows himself to reach a point of near-exhaustion, he may keep the supply at full by quick replacements. These are useful in a variety of ways. All conductors are familiar (Example 20) with the sudden and illogical accentuation of an unimportant syllable at the end of

[10] One of the few devices which may legitimately be brought over from orchestral technique is the slight crescendo which accompanies the release of a final fortissimo chord. This is only possible when the chorus has an adequate breath supply.

a phrase because of the singer's despairing gulp for breath.

EXAMPLE 20

Without a thorough understanding of the principles of breathing, and lacking the will to apply them, a chorus is bound to be defective in one of the important physical bases of group singing.

PHRASING

There is a strong likeness between organ playing and choral singing, and their virtues are to some extent interchangeable. By the same token one of the evils of insensitive organ playing often afflicts choral singing, namely, absence of phrasing. Some organists seem to find it distasteful to remove their hands from the keyboard save for the purpose of changing registration; and some choral conductors never avail themselves of the opportunity to illuminate the text, enhance the musical interest, and, in general, humanize the whole project by calling even for the phrasing that accompanies ordinary conversation, to say nothing of the little lifts and pauses that stimulate interest and add distinction to the singing. For them the only significant punctuation mark is the final period.[11]

Careful pronunciation of final consonants will often, though not invariably, yield all that is necessary by way of phrasing. Where, in the interests of impressiveness, a more marked separation is needed, or where phrasing is difficult because the phrase

[11] Finicky singing is not good singing, and, like any mechanical detail which is so idiomatic that it appears as a superimposed item of technique, it is by no means desirable.

ends with a vowel, the simplest means is to ask the chorus to take a very brief catch-breath, stealing, for this purpose, a fraction from the beat with which the phrase ends. This is illustrated in Examples 21 and 22 (pages 65 and 66). Where a sharply defined consonant is sufficient to mark the phrase-end the sign *v* appears. Where, because of a final vowel or for reasons of emphasis, more distinct "lifts" are needed, I have inserted rests to indicate catch-breaths.[12]

EXAMPLE 21

Another useful type of phrasing consists in shortening the value of the note given to a monosyllable. Single words are in this way often made impressive and the musical interest of a passage emphasized.[13] (See Example 23, page 67.)

Ornamental passages may sometimes be broken up by catch-breaths in such a manner as to add appreciably to clarity, to rhythm, and to the vivacity which is so often inherent in this type of writing (Example 24, page 67).

---

[12] In general, great care should be taken not to slight the note which immediately precedes the catch-breath. That note must receive its full value in tone. In this connection see Example 24 on p. 67.

[13] The singing of the syllable *la* as in *fa la* is often disturbing because of its inappropriate sluggishness. With each repetition of the syllable the tip of the tongue should strike the roof of the mouth and the jaw move freely.

EXAMPLE 22

EXAMPLE 23

EXAMPLE 24

Phrasing, aside from the categorical requirements set by punctuation, is a matter for the conductor's ingenuity. It is based on the principle of silence as effective contrast to sound. As choral conductors we are far too indifferent to the validity of that principle — the prolonged moment which heightens expectation before the first note is heard; the momentary immobility of conductor and chorus which succeeds the final note and prevents the destruction of an impressive occasion by too prompt applause. But far more important are those constantly occurring situations when even the slightest interruption of the music is vital to its effectiveness.

RHYTHM

Rhythmic choral singing is not, in reality, a separate feature of technique. It comes from attention to those details which have already been dealt with, especially the pronunciation of consonants and the interpolated *h*. Only patent artificiality results when any attempt is made to achieve rhythm by marked accentuation or by the employment of purely percussive effects which are a legitimate resource of orchestral music. The rhythmical accentuation of syllables, for example, destroys the reasonableness of the text and reveals the essentially mechanical nature of the usage. Even where inevitability and drive are properly heightened by a very slight accentuation, the chorus, if it is sensitive to the virtue of rhythmic performance as manifested, let us say, in the clear enunciation of consonants, will instinctively supply that stress. The most common instances are to be found in long florid passages which tend either to fall to pieces rhythmically or to be mere melodic decoration. Let me refer again to the "Et resurrexit" (Example 25).

DYNAMICS

It goes without saying that a wide dynamic range is essential; but for once that a conductor feels obliged to ask for more

EXAMPLE 25

volume, he will on twenty occasions ask for less. A fine pianissimo which is maintained at pitch requires mainly a controlled tone and full breathing, and that pianissimo is much easier to produce than a fine fortissimo. Just how loud a chorus may sing without offense is a question each conductor must decide for himself. I would earnestly suggest, however, that no chorus ever be allowed to sing as loud as it can unless it is submerged beneath a sea of orchestral tone. There is, after all, a point at which choral singing ceases to be music and becomes plain natural undisciplined sound. Forte and piano are relative, not abstract terms, and sheer volume is not, in itself, a desideratum.

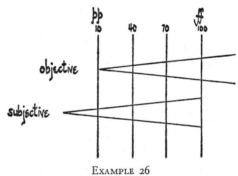

EXAMPLE 26

When I point out the fact that dynamic values are relative, I have in mind the reproach occasionally brought against subjective tone that it makes a real fortissimo impossible. The truth is that the very nature of subjective tone provides a pianissimo which is so shadowy that its quality gives an impression of softness quite unattainable by objective tone; and this makes it unnecessary to force at the other end of the dynamic scale, for by opening the tone slightly when volume is required the resulting contrast in tone color between the very soft and the very loud supplies a dynamic range as wide as that possessed by objective tone. In short, if one set up an arbitrary scale of dynamic values in which 10 represented the objective pianissimo and 100 the subjective fortissimo, the relative distances between the extremes would be practically identical (Example 26).

IMPRESSIVENESS

I am sure that many a beginner, reading the preceding pages of this chapter, will ask whether the best choral singing necessarily requires such meticulous attention to technical matters which involve such a great amount of training in small details. He can answer that question only when he has formulated his own standards of what ideal choral singing should be. I can say for myself that far too much choral singing which I hear seems to me to be quite unimpressive; and I venture to suggest that one reason for the failure of the public to support choral concerts more enthusiastically is that singing of the traditional sort is lacking in the finesse which is an implied feature of professional orchestral playing — not, let me say again, in the type of professional refinement which the trained singer would contribute, but in careful workmanship, which, when applied to amateur choral technique, places the result on a par with professional orchestral performance. My own creed, simply stated, is this: *good choral singing is impossible without unremitting attention to small details, heartlessly, but tactfully, insisted upon.*

Now by impressiveness I mean the effect which the singing creates. It represents the audible sum of the efforts of both conductor and chorus, an element above and beyond any mere objective consideration, such as comprehension of the words or enjoyment of tonal effect taken by themselves. It has to do, in short, with the hearer's *imagination.* Impressive singing is so sincere and spontaneous that the listener feels that every individual performer is actively experiencing the piece; indeed, the performers become for the moment, not agents, but the living voice of the poet and the composer.

Unimpressive singing, on the other hand, suggests a performance in which there is no sense of the singer's personal contribution, but merely of a corporate conveyance of the substance through the services of a musical middleman. The words are conventionally pronounced, and the music is correctly sung; but the result is like expert elocution in which one never feels the heat that generated the original, but only the mild glow that must result from any restatement.

A piece of music in the hands of a chorus may remain just music, or it may become life. Take the "Omnes generationes" from Bach's *Magnificat*. For one group it is a challenge to vigorous and resonant singing; to another it is a drama, the inexorable march of the generations through time, always growing in numbers and in power. The whole panorama of humanity is there; but no chorus, however much it may sense the mightiness of the conception, can make it vivid without the aid of a technique that regards each minute detail. To make of that chorus a *picture* and not a *piece of music* is the prerogative of the chorus that sings impressively; and it is only through such singing that composer, author, chorus, and conductor are duly repaid and the listener rewarded for his interest.

But these compensations are, in a sense, routine. They are intrinsic in any project that is conscientiously carried on, and in the field of music they may be literally wasted unless the substance that gives them life is worthy. The most tragic artistic and educational error that has been committed in this country is the blind assumption that the best is too good; that the enthusiasm of all the participants, including the audience, can be maintained only by the employment of music that is second-rate and attractive only for the moment. That this is untrue has again and again been proved. Yet we, as conductors and music committees, still persist in killing off successive choral enterprises that originated in enthusiasm and high hopes of success, simply because we cannot bring ourselves to believe in the capacity of the average man and woman to respond not to superficial prettiness but to enduring beauty. We descend from appeals to the singers' loyalty to reliance on social and sex distinctions, to suppers after rehearsals, to free tickets for our concerts, and finally we acknowledge a foreordained failure on the ground that "the interest in music is too slight to warrant continuance." Exactly the reverse is true. It is because the singers and the audience are musical that they forsake us; it is because we fail to accept the self-evident fact that a chorus, like any other body that grows by what it feeds on, must have nourishment. Zeal for fine music depends not at all upon education, musical or otherwise. It grows out of an experience of the satisfactions that spring only from association with the highest manifestations of musical art. To initiate this experience, to cultivate it, to enlighten it with technical resource, these are the duty, but still more the privilege, of the conductor.